A Gift for:

_____

From:

_____

Date:

April 4 2000

LIVING
promises

Kenneth Boa

*This book is dedicated
to my wife, Karen,
our daughter, Heather,
our son–in–law, Matthew,
and our new grandson, Kenneth.*

*The LORD bless you and keep you;
The LORD make His face shine upon you,
And be gracious to you;
The LORD lift up His countenance upon you,
And give you peace.*

NUMBERS 6:24–26, NKJV

Introduction

When we contemplate the gracefulness of a flower or the grandeur of a tree, we properly respond with aesthetic admiration. Similarly, we respond to our pets with personal affection, and at times to other people with self–giving love. If nature is worthy of admiration, animals of affection, and human beings of sacrificial love, how then should we respond to the infinite and personal Author of all biological and spiritual life? The biblical answer is clear—God alone is worthy of worship. Blessing and honor and glory and dominion forever belong to the

Creator and Redeemer (REVELATION 5:13), and every tongue in heaven, on earth, and under the earth, including all who have rebelled against Him, will confess this to be so (PHILIPPIANS 2:10–11).

Let us rejoice as we prayerfully reflect on the wonderful promises in Scripture about God's principles, presence, provision, protection, plan, and preparation.

God is preparing a place for me so that I can live with Him forever.

There are many rooms in my Father's house;
I would not tell you this if it were not true.
I am going there to prepare a place for you.
After I go and prepare a place for you,
I will come back and take you to be with me
so that you may be where I am.

JOHN 14:2-3, NCV

Lord Jesus,

Your love and care for me is beyond my imagination.
I can barely comprehend that You have prepared
a special place for me in Your Father's house. As I
pause throughout the day, I will dream of the warmth
and beauty of my heavenly home, and with joy and
excitement, I will anticipate the day when I shall meet
You there and speak with You face to face.

Amen.

God is in control of all things, and He has my best interests at heart.

The LORD is king. He is clothed in majesty.
The LORD is clothed in majesty and armed with strength.
The world is set, and it cannot be moved.
LORD, your kingdom was set up long ago;
you are everlasting. . . .
LORD, your laws will stand forever.
Your Temple will be holy forevermore.

PSALM 93:1-2,5, NCV

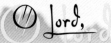

O Lord,

It gives me real comfort to know that Your character never changes and that Your promises stand firm forever. Nothing can thwart Your good plans, and knowing this gives me great assurance in this world of turmoil, change, and uncertainty. My confidence is in Your goodness and majesty.

Amen.

Whatever I do for the sake of Jesus
will not be in vain, but will always endure.

Thanks be to God,
who gives us the victory through
our Lord Jesus Christ.
Therefore I will be steadfast, immovable,
abounding in the work of the Lord,
knowing that my labor in the Lord
is not in vain.

BASED ON 1 CORINTHIANS 15:57-58

Lord,

I am grateful for the victory that You have won for me through my Lord Jesus Christ. Because my life is now in Him, the things I do for His sake will go on into eternity. My labor is not in vain, but will bear lasting fruit as I walk in the power of Your Spirit.

Amen.

Because I am now alive to Christ, I am no longer under the dominion of sin.

If we died with Christ, we know we will also live with him.
Christ was raised from the dead, and we know that
he cannot die again. Death has no power over him now.
Yes, when Christ died, he died to defeat the power of
sin one time—enough for all time. He now has a new life,
and his new life is with God. In the same way,
you should see yourselves as being dead to the power of
sin and alive with God through Christ Jesus.

ROMANS 6:8-11, NCV

14   Week 1, Day 4

Lord Jesus,

It is a marvel that I have died with You and that I will also live with You in the ages to come. May I experience a growing realization that because I am now alive to God in Christ Jesus, I have died to the dominion of sin in my life.

Amen.

The Lord satisfies my spiritual
thirst by inviting me to drink freely
from the water of life.

And He said to me, "It is done!
I am the Alpha and the Omega,
the Beginning and the End.
I will give of the fountain of the water of life
freely to him who thirsts.
He who overcomes shall inherit all things, and
I will be his God and he shall be My son."

REVELATION 21:6-7, NKJV

O Lord,

I rejoice that You are the Alpha and the Omega, the Beginning and the End, and I thank You for Your invitation to drink without cost from the spring of the water of life. May I live in Your strength and lay hold of Your abundant inheritance.

Amen.

*The Lord is my helper and keeper who
watches over my steps and preserves my soul.*

I look up to the hills, but where does my help come from?
My help comes from the LORD, who made heaven and earth.
He will not let you be defeated. He who guards you never sleeps. . . .
The LORD guards you.
The LORD is the shade that protects you from the sun.
The sun cannot hurt you during the day,
and the moon cannot hurt you at night.
The LORD will protect you from all dangers; he will guard your life.
The LORD will guard you as you come and go, both now and forever.

PSALM 121:1-3, 5-8, NCV

Lord,

I look to You for my help and protection in this
uncertain world. You protect me from evil and
preserve my soul. When I suffer pain and loss, even
then I know that You will use it for my ultimate
good by drawing me ever closer to You. My hope is
centered on You and on Your ever–present care.

Amen.

When I come closer to Christ,

He takes my burdens

and gives me His peace.

Come to Me,
all you who labor and are heavy laden,
and I will give you rest.
Take My yoke upon you and learn from Me,
for I am gentle and lowly in heart,
and you will find rest for your souls.
For My yoke is easy and My burden is light.

MATTHEW 11:28-30, NKJV

Lord,

It is only in You that I can find rest for my soul.
When I take Your yoke upon me and learn from You,
I discover the ease of Your yoke and the lightness of
Your burden. Grant me a growing awareness of Your
peace and presence.

Amen.

As I turn from dependence on myself
to dependence on Christ,
I discover His power in my life.

And He said to me, "My grace is sufficient for you,
for My strength is made perfect in weakness."
Therefore most gladly I will rather boast in my infirmities,
that the power of Christ may rest upon me.
Therefore I take pleasure in infirmities, in reproaches,
in needs, in persecutions, in distresses, for Christ's sake.
For when I am weak, then I am strong.

2 CORINTHIANS 12:9-10, NKJV

Lord God,

Teach me to realize that Your grace is always sufficient for me. It is foolish to rely on the weakness of the flesh when I can walk in the power of Christ who lives in me. May I discover His strength by acknowledging my weakness, even in those areas in which I am tempted to think I am competent.

Amen.

Those who serve and follow the Lord will be honored by His presence.

Whoever serves me must follow me.
Then my servant will be with me everywhere I am.
My Father will honor anyone who serves me.

JOHN 12:26, NCV

Lord Jesus,

May I learn to serve You and follow You wherever
You lead me, so that I will abide in You and enjoy
Your manifest presence in my life. I am grateful
that You honor those who serve You. Teach me what
it means to serve You in the daily details of life.

Amen.

The sovereign Lord of creation
rules over all things, and nothing can
thwart His excellent purposes.

The LORD of hosts has sworn, saying,
"Surely, as I have thought, so it shall come to pass,
And as I have purposed, so it shall stand. . . .
For the LORD of hosts has purposed,
And who will annul it?
His hand is stretched out,
And who will turn it back?"

ISAIAH 14:24, 27, NKJV

O Lord,

I revel in the goodness of Your intentions and plans,
knowing that You always desire what is best for Your
people. You rule over all that is in heaven and on earth
and under the earth, and no purpose of Yours can be
annulled. When You stretch out Your hand, nothing
can turn it back.

Amen.

There is no comparison between the afflictions of our brief earthly sojourn and the glory of our eternal heavenly existence.

So we do not give up. Our physical body is becoming older and weaker, but our spirit inside us is made new every day. We have small troubles for a while now, but they are helping us gain an eternal glory that is much greater than the troubles. We set our eyes not on what we see but on what we cannot see. What we see will last only a short time, but what we cannot see will last forever.

2 CORINTHIANS 4:16-18, NCV

Heavenly Father,

Heavenly Father,

The pains and uncertainties of my earthly life sometimes tempt me to lose heart. But when I reflect on the contrast between this momentary light adversity and the endless weight of glory, intimacy, beauty, and adventure in the heavenly realms in Your presence, I am strengthened and encouraged.

Amen.

God Himself will perfect, confirm, strengthen, and establish me in His heavenly kingdom.

The God of all grace,
who called me to His eternal glory in Christ,
after I have suffered a little while,
will Himself perfect, confirm, strengthen,
and establish me.

BASED ON 1 PETER 5:10

God of all grace,

You transmute my very brief suffering on this earth into eternal glory through Your boundless grace and goodness. I will rest in the living hope of the inheritance that You are preparing for those who love You and have come to know You through Your glorious Son.

Amen.

The Lord will reward with the crown of righteousness all who have longed for His appearing.

I will fight the good fight, finish the race,
and keep the faith,
so that there will be laid up for me
the crown of righteousness,
which the Lord, the righteous Judge,
will award to me on that day;
and not only to me, but also to all who
have longed for His appearing.

BASED ON 2 TIMOTHY 4:7-8

Lord,

I know that I am called to fight the good fight and to finish the race You have set before me. May I be faithful and obedient to Your heavenly calling, and may I long more and more for Your glorious appearing as I anticipate seeing You face to face.

Amen.

Those who hunger and thirst
for righteousness
will find satisfaction in Jesus.

Blessed are those who
hunger and thirst for righteousness,
For they shall be filled.

MATTHEW 5:6, NKJV

Lord Jesus,

This world with its constant appeals to vanity, comparison, and earthly wealth is too much with me. Give me the grace to hunger and thirst for the things You declare to be important. May I long for Your righteousness and realize that I possess all things in Christ.

Amen.

God is the source of all pleasure and joy,
and He offers these to all who seek Him.

I have set the LORD always before me;
Because He is at my right hand I shall not be moved.
Therefore my heart is glad, and my glory rejoices;
My flesh also will rest in hope. . . .
You will show me the path of life;
In Your presence is fullness of joy;
At Your right hand are pleasures forevermore.

PSALM 16:8-9, 11, NKJV

Dear Lord,

You are indeed at my right hand, and it is from Your
right hand that I receive the boundless abundance of
Your joy and fullness. I will rest in hope and rejoice in
the glory that You have set before me. Keep me on the
path of life so that I will dwell in Your presence forever.

Amen.

God uses our afflictions to create
a life message that will serve others.

He comforts us every time we have trouble,
so when others have trouble, we can comfort them
with the same comfort God gives us.

2 Corinthians 1:4, ncv

O God,

You have shown me Your tender and severe mercies to train and discipline me in the way of trust, righteousness, and hope so that I will be empowered to minister to others out of my weakness and dependence upon You. May I welcome Your comfort so that I will in turn be able to comfort others.

Amen.

From eternity to eternity,
I am in the great grip of the living God.

God knew them before he made the world, and
he decided that they would be like his Son so that
Jesus would be the firstborn of many brothers.
God planned for them to be like his Son;
and those he planned to be like his Son, he also called;
and those he called; he also made right with him;
and those he made right, he also glorified.

ROMANS 8:29-30, NCV

Dear Lord,

You have foreknown me, chosen me, called me,
and justified me, and You will glorify me in Christ
Jesus. Your purpose is nothing less than that I be fully
conformed to the image of Your Son. May I live in
hope of this great and glorious destiny.

Amen.

All who trust in Jesus have life in His name.

I believe that Jesus is the Christ,
the Son of God,
and by believing,
I have life in His name.

BASED ON JOHN 20:31

Lord,

Thank You for the grace You have shown me by
drawing me to Jesus and enabling me to trust in
Him for the hope of eternal life. I have transferred
my trust from the futility of my own works to the
perfection of His life in me. He is the Anointed
One who came to take away the sin of the world.

Amen.

God is preparing a new heaven
and a new earth
for those who are His own.

Now I saw a new heaven and a new earth,
for the first heaven and the first earth had passed away.
Also there was no more sea.

REVELATION 21:1, NKJV

Lord God,

You have revealed that this present earth and its works
will be burned up, and that You will create a new heaven
and a new earth that will never pass away. May I order
my path in light of this coming new creation so that I
will live in holy conduct and godliness.

Amen.

Because I have trusted in Jesus,
I have eternal life
and will not be condemned.

I tell you the truth, whoever hears what I say
and believes in the One who sent me has eternal life.
That person will not be judged guilty
but has already left death and entered life.

JOHN 5:24, NCV

Lord Jesus,

I have heard Your life-giving Word and entrust myself wholly to You. Thank You for the gift of Your eternal life that dwells in me. And thank You for the realization that I will not face a judgment of condemnation, because my sins have been forgiven and I am a child of the new creation.

Amen.

Whenever God disciplines me, it is for my ultimate good.

Our fathers on earth disciplined us for a short time
in the way they thought was best. But God
disciplines us to help us, so we can become holy as he is.
We do not enjoy being disciplined. It is painful,
but later, after we have learned from it,
we have peace, because we start living in the right way.

HEBREWS 12:10-11, NCV

Lord,

None of us enjoys the painful school of discipline,
but my confidence is in Your good intention to work
this experiential teaching for my good so that I will
grow in Christlike character. This brief period of
earthly discipline will bring forth the eternal fruit
of righteousness.

Amen.

Because of the work of the God-man,
I have been set free from
the bondage caused by the fear of death.

Since these children are people with physical bodies,
Jesus himself became like them. He did this so that,
by dying, he could destroy the one who has the power of
death—the devil—and free those who were like slaves
all their lives because of their fear of death.

HEBREWS 2:14-15, NCV

father,

I thank You that the Lord Jesus has become flesh and blood, so that through His solidarity with the human condition and His glorious victory over the bondage of death, we can be liberated from this slavery and be set free to be God's people of meaning, purpose, and hope.

Amen.

In Christ, I share in the blessings and benefits of the new covenant.

I will put My law in their minds, and write it on their hearts; and I will be their God, and they shall be My people. No more shall every man teach his neighbor, and every man his brother, saying, "Know the LORD," for they all shall know Me, from the least of them to the greatest of them, says the LORD. For I will forgive their iniquity, and their sin I will remember no more.

JEREMIAH 31:33-34, NKJV

Lord,

The beauty and holiness of Your law is beyond human attainment, but because Christ dwells in me, He can live His life through me. May I invite Him to do this each day, so that I will truly know You and walk before You in ways that are pleasing and honoring to You.

Amen.

The Lord is utterly dependable in all the circumstances of life.

The LORD upholds all who fall
and lifts up all who are bowed down.
The eyes of all look to You,
and You give them their food at the proper time.
You open Your hand
and satisfy the desire of every living thing.

BASED ON PSALM 145:14-16

O Lord,

I am grateful that I can always look to You with
confidence and expectant hope. You know my needs
and circumstances, and You continually know and
desire what is best for me. I ask for the grace of
increasing confidence in Your benevolence and power.

Amen.

The living and all-powerful Lord of all creation

invites me to enjoy the rich pleasures of being with Him and knowing Him.

Behold, I stand at the door and knock. If anyone hears
My voice and opens the door, I will come in to him and dine
with him, and he with Me. To him who overcomes I will
grant to sit with Me on My throne, as I also overcame and
sat down with My Father on His throne.

REVELATION 3:20-21, NKJV

Lord Jesus,

You have overcome the power of sin and of death,
and You invite me to welcome You into my innermost
being where I can commune with You. I ask for the
grace to be an overcomer through Your indwelling
power, so that I will have the right to sit with You on
Your throne.

Amen.

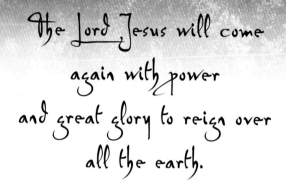

The Lord Jesus will come again with power and great glory to reign over all the earth.

For as the lightning comes from the east and flashes to
the west, so also will the coming of the Son of Man be. . . .
Then the sign of the Son of Man will appear in heaven,
and then all the tribes of the earth will mourn,
and they will see the Son of Man coming on the clouds of
heaven with power and great glory.

MATTHEW 24:27,30, NKJV

Lord Christ,

My firm confidence and expectant hope is in You and in Your glorious promises. I look forward to the consummation of history when You come to establish the fullness of Your kingdom upon the earth. Your kingdom come, Your will be done, on earth as it is in heaven.

Amen.

The God who called us
will also keep us in His loving grip.

God began doing a good work in you,
and I am sure he will continue it until it is finished
when Jesus Christ comes again.

PHILIPPIANS 1:6, NCV

O Lord,

I am glad of the assurance in Your Word that You complete what You have begun. Thank You for choosing and calling me and giving me new life in Christ Jesus, and also for Your promise that You will keep me for the day of redemption when I enter into Your glorious presence.

Amen.

When I received Christ,
I entered into God's eternal family
as a beloved child.

But to all who did accept him and believe in him
he gave the right to become children of God.
They did not become his children in any human way—
by any human parents or human desire.
They were born of God.

JOHN 1:12-13, NCV

Lord Jesus,

I have transferred my trust from myself to You and
have received Your free gift of forgiveness and of eternal
life. Because of Your gift, I have the assurance that I
have become a child of God through the second birth
that comes from above.

Amen.

God is the ever-present and all-sufficient Savior and deliverer of all who take refuge in Him.

The LORD is my rock and my fortress and my deliverer;
The God of my strength, in whom I will trust;
My shield and the horn of my salvation,
My stronghold and my refuge;
My Savior, You save me from violence.
I will call upon the LORD, who is worthy to be praised;
So shall I be saved from my enemies.

2 SAMUEL 22:2-4, NKJV

Lord God,

You alone are my hope and shield and place of refuge.
I have entered into Your stronghold, and in that quiet
place I discover Your presence, peace, and power in
spite of the uncertainties and tempests of this earthly
life. I will call upon You and give You praise, for You
alone are worthy.

Amen.

The Lord is ever-present to strengthen, help, and protect those who call upon Him.

I will not fear, for You are with me;
I will not be dismayed, for You are my God.
You will strengthen me and help me;
You will uphold me with Your righteous right hand. . . .
For You are the LORD my God,
who takes hold of my right hand and says to me,
"Do not fear; I will help you."

BASED ON ISAIAH 41:10, 13

Dear Lord,

It is with gratitude and confidence in Your many mercies that I call upon You in times of peace and times of distress. You have taken hold of my right hand and told me not to fear, for You will help me. Therefore I will not be dismayed or lose hope.

Amen.

God has equipped and empowered me to walk in the new nature I have received in Christ.

As His divine power has given to us all things
that pertain to life and godliness, through the
knowledge of Him who called us by glory and virtue,
by which have been given to us exceedingly great
and precious promises, that through these you may
be partakers of the divine nature, having escaped
the corruption that is in the world through lust.

2 Peter 1:3-4, NKJV

Lord,

It is through Your power that I have become a
partaker of the divine nature, having received the
gift of Christ's indwelling life. You have called
me to this through Your glory and goodness, and
granted me the unbounded riches of Your great
and precious promises.

Amen.

When I live and abide in the love of Jesus, I desire to obey His command to love God and others.

As the Father loved Me, I also have loved you; abide in My love. If you keep My commandments, you will abide in My love, just as I have kept My Father's commandments and abide in His love. These things I have spoken to you, that My joy may remain in you, and that your joy may be full.

John 15:9-11, NKJV

Lord Jesus,

May I revel in Your loving presence and abide in
Your love by living in obedience to the things You
command me to do. May I practice Your presence
in all of my activities and relationships so that
Your joy will become ever more full in my life.

Amen.

Because I believe in Jesus,
I rejoice in the living hope that
I will see Him soon.

Though I have not seen Jesus, I love Him;
and though I do not see Him now but believe in Him,
I rejoice with joy inexpressible and full of glory,
for I am receiving the end of my faith,
the salvation of my soul.

BASED ON 1 PETER 1:8-9

Father,

You have graced me with a love for Jesus even though
I have not yet seen Him. I will continue to hope and
trust in Him in this life, knowing that in the life to
come I will see Him face to face. In this I rejoice as I
await the fullness of my salvation in that glorious day.

Amen.

When we walk in the
light of God's presence,
we are exalted
in His righteousness.

Blessed are the people who know the joyful sound!
They walk, O LORD, in the light of Your countenance.
In Your name they rejoice all day long,
And in Your righteousness they are exalted.

PSALM 89:15-16, NKJV

Lord God,

May I rejoice in Your name throughout the day
and order my steps as if I could see You. Let me
walk in the light of Your presence and learn
to acclaim You in thought, word, and deed. Then
I will be exalted in Your righteousness, and my
joy will continue to increase.

Amen.

In Christ, I am destined to receive a kingdom that cannot be shaken.

Therefore, since we are receiving a kingdom
which cannot be shaken, let us have grace,
by which we may serve God acceptably with reverence
and godly fear. For our God is a consuming fire.

HEBREWS 12:28-29, NKJV

My God,

I want to worship You acceptably with reverence and awe, for You are a consuming fire of holiness and love. Teach me to be ever more thankful, so that growing gratitude will be my worship as I remember Your radiant promise that I am destined in Christ to receive a kingdom that can never be overthrown or diminished.

Amen.

Because I am in Christ, God has implanted His light, glory, and power within me.

God once said, "Let the light shine out of the darkness!" This is the same God who made his light shine in our hearts by letting us know the glory of God that is in the face of Christ. We have this treasure from God, but we are like clay jars that hold the treasure. This shows that the great power is from God, not from us.

2 CORINTHIANS 4:6-7, NCV

O God,

Although I formerly was darkness, now I am light in the Lord. You have given me the light of the knowledge of Your glory in the face of Your Son, and this treasure becomes most evident when I walk in dependence on Your power and not on my own.

Amen.

Because I believe in the name of the Son of God, I know that I have eternal life.

This is what God told us: God has given us eternal life, and this life is in his Son. Whoever has the Son has life, but whoever does not have the Son of God does not have life. I write this letter to you who believe in the Son of God so you will know you have eternal life.

1 John 5:11-13, NCV

Lord God,

I thank You for the boundless and costly gift of
eternal life that was purchased by the redemptive
work of Your Son. Because I have come to believe
in His name, I have Your assurance that I have
eternal life in Him. May I live and walk in His life
and display it to others.

Amen.

Because the Lord is the strength of my life, I need fear no one.

The LORD is my light and my salvation;
Whom shall I fear?
The LORD is the strength of my life;
Of whom shall I be afraid?

PSALM 27:1, NKJV

O Lord,

You are my light and my salvation, and it is in
You that my real strength resides. Because of Your
empowering presence, I will not be fearful or dismayed.
When I am anxious, I will turn my burdens over
to You and replace earthly fear with divine peace.

Amen.

When I approach You by asking,
seeking, and knocking,
I have Your assurance that
You will respond.

When I ask, it will be given to me; when I seek, I will find;
when I knock, the door will be opened to me.
For everyone who asks receives; he who seeks finds;
and to him who knocks, the door will be opened.

BASED ON MATTHEW 7:7-8 & LUKE 11:9-10

Lord,

I come to You in full acknowledgement of my desperation and need for You. I am grateful that You open the door upon which I knock, and that You reward those who seek You. In Your grace You give me better than what I request, because You alone know what I truly need.

Amen.

I can be confident that God will answer my prayers when I trust in Him.

So I tell you to believe that you have received the things you ask for in prayer, and God will give them to you.

MARK 11:24, NCV

Lord,

May I walk in Your will and desire the things
You desire for me. I will delight myself in You
and ask without wavering in doubt and disbelief,
trusting in Your boundless resources and in Your
willingness to give me what is best.

Amen.

In Christ, I have a source of peace that the world cannot give.

Peace I leave with you,
My peace I give to you;
not as the world gives do I give to you.
Let not your heart be troubled,
neither let it be afraid.

JOHN 14:27, NKJV

Dear Lord,

I will revel and rejoice in the transcendent peace
that You alone can give to me. Because I have hoped
and trusted in Jesus, I need never be troubled and
fearful. You have given me an inner peace that the
world can neither understand nor offer.

Amen.

Having confessed and believed in the Lord Jesus, I am saved and will never be put to shame.

If you confess with your mouth the Lord Jesus
and believe in your heart that God has raised Him from
the dead, you will be saved. For with the heart one
believes unto righteousness, and with the mouth confession
is made unto salvation. For the Scripture says,
"Whoever believes on Him will not be put to shame."

ROMANS 10:9-11 NKJV

90   Week 7, Day 6

Lord Jesus,

I have trusted in You with my heart and confessed
You before others with my mouth. Knowing
that You are wholly trustworthy, I will never be
put to shame, but continue on the way of
righteousness and salvation until I stand before
You, holy and blameless.

Amen.

God fully provides for all my needs according to His glorious riches in Christ Jesus.

My God will use his wonderful riches in
Christ Jesus to give you everything you need.
Glory to our God and Father forever and ever! Amen.

PHILIPPIANS 4:19-20, NCV

Father,

My hope for every form of provision—physical,
emotional, relational, financial—is solely founded
on Your promises and power. You fully know me
and all of my needs, and I look with confidence to
Your abundant provision of every good thing that
will lead to life and godliness.

Amen.

The God who is there rewards those who earnestly seek Him.

Without faith no one can please God.
Anyone who comes to God must believe that he is real and
that he rewards those who truly want to find him.

HEBREWS 11:6, NCV

Lord God,

May I please You through a growing faith and
confidence in Your goodness, greatness, grace, and
glory. Not only do You exist, but You are the source
of all that is. I will earnestly seek You, knowing
that You always reward those who pursue You.

Amen.

In Christ, I am destined to receive a glorified resurrection body.

But our homeland is in heaven,
and we are waiting for our Savior,
the Lord Jesus Christ, to come from heaven.
By his power to rule all things,
he will change our simple bodies and make
them like his own glorious body.

PHILIPPIANS 3:20-21, NCV

Lord,

I eagerly look forward to the coming of the Lord
Jesus Christ, who will subject all things in the
created order to Himself. In that day, I will receive
a resurrected body that will be glorious and perfect,
because it will be conformed to Jesus' glorious body.

Amen.

God is our refuge and fortress, and we can rest in Him.

He who dwells in the secret place of the Most High
Shall abide under the shadow of the Almighty.
I will say of the LORD, "He is my refuge and my fortress;
My God, in Him I will trust."

PSALM 91:1-2, NKJV

Lord God Almighty,

I thank You that You have become my refuge
and fortress, and that I can rest in the shadow of the
Almighty. You are the Most High, the Almighty,
the Lord, and my God in whom I trust. I will not
be fearful but confident, knowing that nothing can
separate me from Your love and power.

Amen.

As a member of God's flock,
I have the gift of eternal life,
and no one can snatch
me from the Father's grip.

My sheep listen to my voice; I know them, and they
follow me. I give them eternal life, and they will never die,
and no one can steal them out of my hand. My Father
gave my sheep to me. He is greater than all, and no person
can steal my sheep out of my Father's hand.

JOHN 10:27-29, NCV

Father,

By Your grace, I have heard Your voice and am a member of Your flock. You have given me eternal life, and I will never perish or be separated from You. You hold me in Your hand, and I delight to follow You.

Amen.

The Spirit of God who raised Jesus from the dead lives in me and will raise me from the dead.

Your body will always be dead because of sin.
But if Christ is in you, then the Spirit gives you life,
because Christ made you right with God.
God raised Jesus from the dead, and if God's Spirit is
living in you, he will also give life to your bodies that die.
God is the One who raised Christ from the dead,
and he will give life through his Spirit that lives in you.

ROMANS 8:10-11, NCV

Lord,

I give thanks that although my body is mortal,
my spirit is alive with the indwelling Holy Spirit.
And it is through the power of Your Holy Spirit
that I will be raised from the dead so that I will be
made complete in my spirit, soul, and body.

Amen.

The Holy Spirit has been given to me as a guarantee
that my mortality will be swallowed up by life.

I know that if my earthly house, or tent, is destroyed,
I have a building from God,
a house not made with hands, eternal in the heavens.
For in this house I groan, longing to be clothed
with my heavenly dwelling,
because when I am clothed, I will not be found naked.
For while I am in this tent, I groan, being burdened,
because I do not want to be unclothed but to be clothed,
so that what is mortal may be swallowed up by life.
Now it is God who has made me for this very purpose
and has given me the Spirit as a guarantee.

BASED ON 2 CORINTHIANS 5:1-5

O Lord,

I groan in my mortal corruption, knowing that
my earthly body is frail and temporary. I await the
day when I will be clothed with an eternal dwelling
that will display Your glory and will never be
corrupted or diminished.

Amen.

When I abide in Jesus,

I experience the joy of answered prayer.

If I abide in You, and Your words abide in me,
I can ask whatever I wish, and it will be done for me.
As I ask in Your name, I will receive, that my joy may be full.

BASED ON JOHN 15:7 & JOHN 16:24

Lord Jesus,

I know that when I abide in You and let Your
words abide in me, the things I desire are also the
things that You would be pleased to grant. In these
times I can approach You with confidence, knowing
that I will receive what I ask in Your name.

Amen.

Faith is the victory that overcomes the world, and my faith is in the person and work of the Son of God.

Everyone who believes that Jesus is the Christ is God's child, and whoever loves the Father also loves the Father's children. . . . Because everyone who is a child of God conquers the world. And this is the victory that conquers the world—our faith. So the one who wins against the world is the person who believes that Jesus is the Son of God.

1 JOHN 5:1, 4-5, NCV

Father,

I have come to believe that Jesus is the Christ,
Your only begotten Son. This is the faith that
empowers me to overcome the world. In Him
I have received the new birth, and I have come
to love You and Your Son.

Amen.

My security is in the Lord who will bring me safely to His heavenly kingdom.

The Lord will deliver me from every
evil work and preserve me for His heavenly kingdom.
To Him be glory forever and ever. Amen!

2 TIMOTHY 4:18, NKJV

Lord,

My confidence rests entirely on You and not myself.
I know that You will deliver me from all evil intentions
and devices, and that You will bring me safely in the
end to Your heavenly kingdom. There I will behold
Your resplendent glory for ever.

Amen.

The Lord is preparing joys
beyond earthly imagination for
those who love Him.

Eye has not seen, nor ear heard,
Nor have entered into the heart of man
The things which God has prepared for those who love Him.

1 CORINTHIANS 2:9, NKJV

Dear God,

Dear God,

I do not possess the mental capacity to begin to
imagine what You are preparing to give to Your
children. The greatest beauties that I have seen
or heard or read about are as nothing in comparison
to the eternal ecstasy of being immersed in Your
triune glory.

Amen.

The worst pains I will experience
in this life

are as nothing in comparison to the
glory that is to come.

If children, then heirs—heirs of God and
joint heirs with Christ, if indeed we suffer with Him,
that we may also be glorified together.
For I consider that the sufferings of this present time
are not worthy to be compared
with the glory which shall be revealed in us.

ROMANS 8:17-18, NKJV

O Lord,

This brief earthly existence is fraught with hardships and disappointments, but I know that even these will contribute to the glory to come. As a joint heir with Christ, I will receive that which will endure forever and will never fade away.

Amen.

In Christ I have a living hope of an unfading inheritance.

Blessed be the God and Father of our
Lord Jesus Christ, who according to His abundant
mercy has begotten us again to a living hope
through the resurrection of Jesus Christ from the dead,
to an inheritance incorruptible and undefiled and
that does not fade away, reserved in heaven for you.

1 PETER 1:3-4, NKJV

Father God,

I bless You indeed because of Your great mercy and because of my new birth into a living hope. In Christ, my inheritance will never be corrupted, defiled, or diminished. It is reserved in heaven for me, and I will enjoy the blessings of Your presence in the ages to come.

Amen.

God has plans to give me a future and a hope.

"I know what
I am planning for you," says the LORD.
"I have good plans for you,
not plans to hurt you.
I will give you hope and a good future."

JEREMIAH 29:11, NCV

O Lord,

I give thanks that You are my unchanging source
of meaning and hope, and that I am here for a purpose.
Because of Your great love, and because You are in
control of all things, nothing will defeat Your gracious
plans to give me a future and a hope.

Amen.

God is the help of my countenance and the restorer of my soul.

Why are you cast down, O my soul?
And why are you disquieted within me?
Hope in God, for I shall yet praise Him
For the help of His countenance.
O my God, my soul is cast down within me;
Therefore I will remember You . . .
Why are you cast down, O my soul?
And why are you disquieted within me?
Hope in God;
For I shall yet praise Him,
The help of my countenance and my God.

PSALM 42:5-6, 11, NKJV

Lord God,

When I am downcast and disturbed, may I quickly
turn to You and hold fast to Your perfect character.
May I practice Your presence in all things and at
all times, so that I will walk in Your peace and power
in trying times. I will praise You for the help of
Your presence.

Amen.

The more I walk in loving obedience to Jesus,
the greater my fellowship
with the Father and the Son.

Those who know my commands
and obey them are the ones who love me,
and my Father will love those who love me.
I will love them and will show myself to them.

JOHN 14:21, NCV

Lord Jesus,

I ask for the grace to respond to Your Word with
a heart of obedience that is prompted by love. I
desire a growing manifestation of You and the Father
in my life, and I wish to walk in responsiveness to
all that You desire me to be and to do.

Amen.

My life is hidden with Christ in God, and I will appear with Him in glory.

Since I have been raised with Christ,
I should seek the things above,
where Christ is seated at the right hand of God.
I will set my mind on the things above,
not on the things on the earth,
for I died, and my life is now hidden with Christ in God.
When Christ who is my life appears,
then I also will appear with Him in glory.

BASED ON COLOSSIANS 3:1-4

Lord Christ,

You are in me, and I am in You. I choose to believe
that I am seated at the right hand of the Father
with You, even though this is contrary to my feelings
and experiences. In this life I walk by faith, but the
day is coming when I will appear with You in glory.

Amen.

I have confidence that I will receive
whatever I ask that is according
to the will of Jesus.

Now this is the confidence that we have in Him,
that if we ask anything according to His will,
He hears us. And if we know that He hears us,
whatever we ask, we know that we
have the petitions that we have asked of Him.

1 JOHN 5:14-15, NKJV

Lord, Jesus,

May my prayers be in accordance with Your will,
so that I will grow in grace and in intimacy with
You. I give thanks for answered prayer, knowing
that You care about the things that concern
me and that You are pleased when I come to You
with my requests.

Amen.

Kenneth Boa is engaged in a ministry of relational evangelism and discipleship, teaching, writing, and speaking. He holds a B.S. from Case Institute of Technology, a Th.M. from Dallas Theological Seminary, a Ph.D. from New York University, and a D.Phil. from the University of Oxford in England.

He is the President of Reflections Ministries, an organization that seeks to encourage, teach, and equip people to know Christ, follow Him, become progressively conformed to His image, and reproduce His life in others.

Dr. Boa writes a free monthly teaching letter called *Reflections*. If you would like to be on the mailing list, visit www.reflectionsministries.org or call 800–DRAW NEAR (800–372–9632).